GREAT DANES

BIG DOGS

by Allan Morey

Content Consultant: Sarah K. Crain
Doctor of Veterinary Medicine
Tufts University
North Grafton, Massachusetts

Pebble® Plus

CAPSTONE PRESS
a capstone imprint

Pebble Plus is published by Capstone Press,
1710 Roe Crest Drive, North Mankato, Minnesota 56003
www.mycapstone.com

Library of Congress Cataloging-in-Publication Data
Names: Morey, Allan, author.
Title: Great Danes / by Allan Morey.
Description: North Mankato, Minnesota : Capstone Press, a Capstone imprint,
   2016. | ?2016 | Series: Big dogs | Audience: Ages 5-7.? | Audience: K to
   grade 3.? | Includes bibliographical references and index.
Identifiers: LCCN 2015030279 | ISBN 9781491479780 (library binding)
Subjects: LCSH: Great Dane--Juvenile literature. | Dog breeds--Juvenile
   literature.
Classification: LCC SF429.G7 M67 2016 | DDC 636.73--dc23
LC record available at http://lccn.loc.gov/2015030279

Editorial Credits
Nikki Bruno Clapper, editor; Juliette Peters, designer;
Morgan Walters, media researcher; Katy LaVigne, production specialist

Photo Credits
Dreamstime: Szabolcs Stieber, 15; Getty Images: Siri Stafford, 5; iStockphoto: Chris Bernard
Photography Inc., 21; Newscom: Steimer, C./picture alliance/Arco Images G, 9; Shutterstock:
andrewvec, (speedometer) cover, Dmussman, 19, Elsa Hoffmann, 11, Eric Isselee, 1, (dog) bottom
left 22, gvictoria, 17, Hywit Dimyadi, (dog silouette) cover, jacotakepics, cover, kostolom3000, (dog
head) backcover, 3, MF Photo, 13, pixshots, 7, Stephaniellen, (elephant) bottom right 22, vlastas,
(paw prints) design element throughout

Note to Parents and Teachers

The Big Dogs set supports national science standards related to life science. This book describes
and illustrates Great Danes. The images support early readers in understanding the text. The
repetition of words and phrases helps early readers learn new words. This book also introduces
early readers to subject-specific vocabulary words, which are defined in the Glossary section. Early
readers may need assistance to read some words and to use the Table of Contents, Glossary, Read
More, Internet Sites, Critical Thinking Using the Common Core, and Index sections of the book.

Printed in the United States of America in North Mankato, Minnesota.
102015   009221CGS16

Table of Contents

GENTLE GIANTS

People call Great Danes gentle giants. These dogs are big and strong. They are also sweet family pets.

Great Danes were bred as working dogs. People used them to guard their homes. Great Danes are loyal and obedient.

Today most Great Danes
are pets. They are good with
children and other animals.
They are also very playful.

ROYAL DOGS

Great Danes look royal,
like kings and queens.
Their necks and bodies
are long. They hold their
heads proudly.

A Great Dane's body
is strong and muscular.
But these dogs move
gracefully. Great Danes
live for 7 to 10 years.

CARING FOR A GREAT DANE

Training is important for Great Danes because of their size. If they jump on you, they might knock you over!

Great Danes are indoor dogs.
Their coats are too short
for cold weather. These dogs
like to curl up in soft,
comfortable beds.

Great Danes do not run around a lot. But they still need a couple of short walks each day. You can also let them play in a fenced yard.

Great Danes make great
house pets. But remember,
they need lots of space.
You might find a big dog
in your bed!

GLOSSARY

breed—to mate and produce young

coat—an animal's hair or fur

gentle—kind and calm

loyal—being true to something or someone

obedient—able to follow rules and commands

royal—having to do with a king or queen

train—to teach an animal to do what you say

working dog—a dog that is bred to do a job, such as guarding homes or herding animals

HOW BIG ARE THEY?

	Great Dane	Baby Elephant
Average Height	28–34 inches (71–86 centimeters)	36 inches (91 cm)
Average Weight	110–175 pounds (50–79 kilograms)	200 pounds (91 kg)

READ MORE

Johnson, Jinny. *Great Dane.* My Favorite Dogs. Mankato, Minn.: A+, Smart Apple Media, 2015.

Rajczak, Kristen. *Great Danes.* Great Big Dogs. New York: Gareth Stevens Pub., 2012.

Shores, Erika L. *Pet Dogs Up Close.* Pebble Plus: Pets Up Close. North Mankato, Minn.: Capstone Press, 2015.

INTERNET SITES

FactHound offers a safe, fun way to find Internet sites related to this book. All of the sites on FactHound have been researched by our staff.

Here's all you do:

Visit *www.facthound.com*

Type in this code: 9781491479780

Check out projects, games and lots more at
www.capstonekids.com

23

CRITICAL THINKING
USING THE COMMON CORE

1. Why do you think Great Danes would be good guard dogs?
   (Key Ideas and Details)

2. Families should choose a pet that is right for them.
   What do you like about Great Danes?
   What might make them hard to own?
   (Integration of Knowledge and Ideas)

INDEX